Mary Magdalene:

A Mystery Play

Mary Magdalene:

A Mystery Play

by

SHEILAH R CRAFT

STARLIGHT BOOKS

STARLIGHT BOOKS

This Mystery Play is a work of the author's imagination, even though it is inspired by the King James Version of the Holy Bible. Some characters are used fictiously; other characters are the creation of the author, and any resemblance to actual persons, living or dead, is purely coincidental.

Copyright © 1994, 2012 by Sheilah R Craft

All rights reserved, including the right to reproduce this book or portions thereof in any form whatsoever, except for brief quotations for review purposes.

This play is registered with the United States Library of Congress.

First Starlight Books edition November 2012

ISBN-13: 978-0-615-72183-5

ISBN-10: 0615721834

PREFACE

Foremost among the list of religious and theological works which must be consulted for historical background, in the writing of such a work as this play, is, of course, the Bible. Of specific note are the Gospels: Matthew, Mark, Luke, and John. These books are the orthodox Gospels of Christianity.

However, when composing the life of one about whom so little historical knowledge is revealed--Mary Magdalene--it is necessary to refer to other sources as well. These sources would naturally include the Gnostic gospels, especially the gospels of Mary, Philip, Thomas, and the Dialogue of the Savior. When taken in conjunction with the orthodox Gospels, one is given a fuller understanding of the importance of Mary Magdalene in the story of Jesus, especially in regards to the Resurrection.

Gnostic gospels were considered heretical by the orthodox community, for they claimed to contain mystical communications from, and therefore mystical communion with, Jesus. These gospels would make the recipient of this communication, or communion, the focus--and oftentimes this person was one outside the Twelve (the chosen disciples), such as Mary Magdalene. These people, the Gnostics claimed, received their divine communications via visions in which they saw Jesus. Through these visions, He would impart to them divine knowledge or revelation. This divine knowledge was given only to them, not to the Twelve. The implication that the Gnostics were therefore set apart and favored over the orthodox Twelve caused much outcry, dissent, and controversy between the two groups: the Gnostics and the orthodox community.

Nevertheless, controversy aside, the orthodox and the Gnostic gospels work hand-in-hand to emphasize the unique position of Mary Magdalene--as the recipient not only of divine healing, but of the first sight of the risen Jesus. Of specific interest is the fact that the Gnostic gospels are supported by the orthodox Gospels--each set reveals in their texts that Mary Magdalene understood what the disciples did not at that point understand: that Jesus was the true Messiah and had risen from the tomb as He had revealed He would. When Mary relates her encounter at the tomb to the disciples, they mostly doubt her. In the Gnostic gospels, it is Peter and Andrew who verbally reveal their disbelief at the words of Mary Magdalene, and it is Levi who, standing alone among them, defends her.

Throughout history, numerous theological texts have discussed the Gospels, the role of women in Jesus' life, and the Resurrection. I have consulted several books representative of this scholarship, books which not only support Mary Magdalene's important and unequaled role, but which offer fresh insight on the subject of Christianity in general.

Many authors have, as well, composed biographies of Jesus or of those closest to Him. I have, in addition to the other sources mentioned, read representatives of these, specifically biographies of Jesus and the Virgin Mary. In each of them, Mary Magdalene was a prominent character. These books served not only as companion pieces to the gospels and the theological texts, but served to illustrate the artistic, or creative, representation of a biblical figure by an author--which is the very task that I faced in approaching this project.

Biblical personages have proven to be a favorite subject for hundreds of artists throughout the centuries, as well. And, while a writer tends to paint her own mental portraits of the characters she writes about, the many images of Mary Magdalene were entertaining and enlightening, revealing how she has been viewed at different points in history.

While each source I consulted proved invaluable in its own way, the end result is a combination of each of them, with a large dose of artistic, or poetic, license, as well as personal faith, thrown amongst them. The characters are almost all based on historical figures: Mary Magdalene, Jesus, Peter, and Levi. Only the character of Jonathan is of my own creation; he proved to be the tool by which the different aspects of the Mary Magdalene story could be tied together in such a way that her story as a whole becomes the backdrop for the Resurrection itself. In relating her story to Jonathan, in telling him of her firsthand experiences, Mary Magdalene is really teaching the basic doctrines of Jesus' earthly ministry. Mary Magdalene is fulfilling what was to be Jesus' command to His disciples: to witness for Him to all they meet. In doing so, Mary is also the first female evangelist. The words spoken by the characters are also original. Only the words of Jesus, in the last scenes of the play, are not; they are quoted directly from the King James Bible.

The finished work should relay the message which the Bible, and each of the other sources, carry: that Mary Magdalene was a converted sinner; that she was a woman in

MARY MAGDALENE: A MYSTERY PLAY

(spiritual) love with her Lord; that she was a woman who understood, more so than did the disciples, that Jesus was indeed the Messiah and what that truly meant; and that she remembered and understood His words to them concerning the Resurrection. Therefore, she was rewarded by being the first person to be visited by the risen Christ. The disciples, when told of her encounter, largely doubt her claims; only when Christ appears to them, and they see Him for themselves, do they believe in the Resurrection. It is then, too, that they realize that Mary Magdalene had, indeed, been correct.

DEDICATED TO

NANCY SPARKS,

WHO ENCOURAGED

ME TO PUBLISH THIS PLAY

AND TO THUS SPREAD THE WORD

Jesus said unto her, I am the resurrection, and the life: he that believeth in me, though he were dead, yet shall he live:

--JOHN 11:25

MARY MAGDELENE: A MYSTERY PLAY

SETTING:

SCENES I & II:

THE GARDEN, ON THE THIRD DAY AFTER THE CRUCIFIXION OF JESUS. SEVERAL TREES AND LARGE ROCKS POPULATE THE GARDEN; MARY MAGDALENE IS SITTING UNDER A TREE, LEANING AGAINST A ROCK THERE, DURING SCENE I AND THE OPENING OF SCENE II. BEHIND HER IS A WALL OF STONE AND ROCK; AN OPENING IN THE WALL HAS BEEN COVERED WITH A LARGE, FLAT STONE. THIS IS THE TOMB OF JESUS. THE STONE HAS BEEN ROLLED AWAY, REVEALING THE OPENING, AT THE BEGINNING OF SCENE II.

SCENES III & IV:

A NONDESCRIPT HOUSE WHERE THE TWELVE DISCIPLES HAVE BEEN RESIDING. INSIDE, A LARGE ROOM OCCUPIES THE BOTTOM PORTION OF THE DWELLING, FURNISHED WITH ONLY A ROUGH-HEWN WOODEN TABLE AND CHAIRS. A LADDER FASHIONED FROM TREE LIMBS LEADS TO A LOFT ABOVE, WHICH CONTAINS ONLY HAY, STRAW, AND A FEW WORN BLANKETS, AND IS THE SLEEPING QUARTERS OF THE TWELVE MEN.

MARY MAGDALENE: A MYSTERY PLAY

CAST:

MARY MAGDALENE, A YOUNG VIRGIN.

JONATHAN . . . . AGED 15.

ANGELS, TWO MESSENGERS OF GOD, WHOSE COUNTENANCES ARE FULL OF BRIGHT, WHITE LIGHT.

JESUS . . . . AGED 33.

PETER, A FISHER WHO HAD BEEN CALLED BY JESUS TO BE A DISCIPLE.

LEVI, A PUBLICAN WHO BECAME A DISCIPLE AT JESUS' COMMAND.

TIME:

30 A.D.

SCENE I

IN THE GARDEN, NEAR THE SEPULCHRE WHERE JESUS WAS LATELY ENTOMBED. IT IS NOW QUIET, AS ALL WHO HAD BEEN PRESENT ARE NOW AGONE. ONE LONE FIGURE REMAINS IN THE GARDEN, SITTING BENEATH A TREE. NOW ONE PASSING NEARBY SEES THAT THIS WOMAN IS ALONE, AND THAT SHE APPEARS TO BE GRIEVED, AND SO COMES NEAR TO HER.

JONATHAN: Woman, what ails ye?

MARY MAGDALENE: (looking up at him) I have lost the most important man of my life. He is gone from this world.

JONATHAN: I am indeed very sorely aggrieved for ye. Pray tell me, was this man thine father, or thine brother, or perhaps thine husband?

MARY MAGDALENE: This man, he was all of those people to me, and, lo, more beside.

JONATHAN: (confused) Forgive me if perhaps I appear ignorant of what thou sayest, but . . .how is it that one man can be thine father, and thine brother, and thine husband?

MARY MAGDALENE: For him 'twas quite simple, sith he was born in order to be everyone to all people.

JONATHAN: Who was this man whom ye claim to be so very . . . .

(He ceases to speak when he sees the look of pain upon Mary Magdalene's face.)

MARY MAGDALENE: His name was Jesus. He was the most wonderful man who has ever lived.

JONATHAN: Tell me about him.

MARY MAGDALENE: It so happened that in my youth I had been cursed by seven demons, which continued to plague mine body and mine spirit for many a year. I did have the bountiful and kindly friendship of Joanna, whom I had shared the years of childhood with in Magdala. 'Twas Joanna who heard from her husband Chuza, (a man of much importance, as he was the steward to Herod Antipas,) of this man called Jesus, and of the wondrous and miraculous works he had done throughout the land, and that he was to pass near to Magdala on his way from Capernaum. So 'twas that Joanna yearned to take me to this man. And so she did. I remember being affrightened as she led me to him, as he came into the city, and a great multitude thronged around him, yelling and begging and screaming and praying for him to save them, to heal them, to touch them. I was so affrightened, for, you understand, I was filled with the evil and unclean spirits of the devil's design; these spirits, they did not care for any person, or any place, or anything which was divine and holy of nature. And Jesus is, you see, the most divine and the most holy of all people.

JONATHAN: Forgive me yet anew, but I am indeed astonied. How is it that now thou sayest that this man is the most divine and the most holy of all people, when thou hast said beforetime that this man Jesus is dead. Do to wit what 'tis thou meanest to say, woman. There is no man can remain divine and holy, when he is yet dead. 'Tis not meet that it should be thus.

MARY MAGDALENE: I am indeed fain to be obedient to thy request. But thou must needs be patient, and thou shalt understand it all by the by. It shall be made clear to thee.

MARY MAGDALENE: A MYSTERY PLAY

JONATHAN: Very well. I shall listen. Pray continue.

MARY MAGDALENE: Well, so 'twas that Joanna brought me to this man, this great teacher and healer. And she approached near to him and asked him to heal me of the seven demons which had plagued me sith mine youth. This man did look upon me as I did stand afore him, the spirits yet making me to cower in fear; he did look upon me, and he did smile, and his smile was filled with such love and with such tenderness, that it did make the spirits within me, yea, all the more affrightened. Then he touched me. He touched me, and, lo, the seven spirits departed from within me, and I was made whole yet again. His hands were filled with such warmth that mine entire body was imbued with that warmth. I was indeed grateful to this man, for he had done what no one else had ever been able to do: he had saved me from the clutches of Satan. I looked up into his eyes, and, lo, a more beautiful sight one could never dream possible. Those eyes were filled with such love and kindness and . . . holiness. Mine own eyes shed tears merely to look into them. I wist then, in that selfsame moment, that I would follow him forevermore. That very moment I did find what had been absent from mine life for so many long years: I found a love so pure, so true, so unfailing, that I had no choice, nay, none, but to return it an hundredfold. Jesus would, from that very moment onward, become the center of mine existence on this earth of God the Father's creation.

JONATHAN: Dost thou meanest to say that thou left thine home and thine family to follow this man, this man that thou had only just come to know?

MARY MAGDALENE: My son, I was alone in this world, but for my dear friend Joanna and the servants of mine home, mine parents being long afore dead of this world. I was alone, yea, completely and utterly alone, with none to love me, and none for to give my love to. I followed Jesus and his disciples, for he had given me the most wondrous of gifts: he gave me my soul and my salvation and the forgiveness which is so precious that it can be found only in him and in his Father.

JONATHAN: I wit that thou wert indeed grateful to this Jesus for what he had done for thee. But, woman, was not that a very foolish thing for thee to do, to follow a stranger and his men, thou being a virgin alone? Didst thou not fear for thy safety and for thy reputation? Knowest thou not that thou couldst have been readily charged with being an harlot by the people, and that thou wouldst surely then have been stoned to death?

MARY MAGDALENE: Thou dost not yet understand, but thou shalt surely understand afore I am finished. 'Twas not foolish of me to devote mineself completely to Jesus, for his work on this earth was of the utmost importance. I had no need to fear the wrath nor the judgment of the people, for

Jesus and his Father know my heart and my spirit, and that is all that doth matter. What people say or yet even think about us should now concern us, so long as our hearts and our spirits are right with God. Nay, I feared the people not, nor did I need fear for myself, for I could never wish to be safer than I was in the company of Jesus. Nor did I need fear his disciples, for we were all of us committed to Jesus, to helping him and to caring for him.

(Her voice drops to a mere whisper.)

Yea, and we are still yet committed to him.

JONATHAN: Might I ask of thee what 'twas that Jesus did?

MARY MAGDALENE: But of course. You see, my son, he did for many hundreds, nay thousands, of people, what he had done for me: he healed people, he saved people, he taught people, lo, he even raised from death's sleep, many of those people who had given up the spirit. He did many great and wondrous things. He worked many miracles during his time among man.

JONATHAN: And thou sawest these 'miracles'?

MARY MAGDALENE: Yea, but of course. Dost thou forget that I did not only witness the miracles, but that, lo, I did receive a miracle mineself? How else dost thou explain the purging of mine soul from the seven demons? By the touch of his anointed hands, by the touch of those hands and by no other means excepting that, was I made free from sin. Those of us who went with him, the twelve disciples and those of us who ministered unto him, were witness to many things which Jesus did for the many thousands who came before him, begging for a miracle for themselves or for one dear to them. And those thousands of people who were alway surrounding him, they too were witness to a great many of the miracles which Jesus did perform. 'Twas them that did spread both far and wide throughout the land the news of Jesus and his great works; 'twas how the husband of Joanna did come to hear of and thus tell her of him, and how she therefore did come to bring me before him. 'T did appear to seem that wheresoever Jesus did go to, the people there had already heard word of him, and so many thousands would gather about him, longing either to receive a miracle or else to witness his works with their own eyes. Many hundreds   of thousands were thusly healed or saved or raised from death; all who witnessed his works and believed on him were changed as was I.

JONATHAN: Could it be that this Jesus of yours was the great prophet and rabbi of which we heard tell as we passed on our journey here for the feast of the Passover? There were many who told of a man filled with such power that he was thus able to heal men of blindness, and many other such ailments, and that he spoke of the will and the laws of God.

MARY MAGDALENE: Yea, the people you did hear did indeed speak of Jesus. Wilt thou permit me to inquire as to whether thou didst believe the words these people did speak?

JONATHAN: (He looks down in shame, speaking softly.) Nay, I did not believe their words. For it seemed too much of the nature of an idle tale to be truthful. We . . . I, I did not believe it possible that a man could do what the people were saying that this Jesus had done. (He pauses, then looks at Mary, tears in his eyes.) But now I do believe. I cannot doubt thee, for I have but to look upon thine eyes and thy face for to see the love and the truth in thee. I must admit that I have never seen such a love afore; thy face doth glow with it, thine eyes do shine with it. Indeed, thy whole countenance doth radiate with thy love and thy gratitude. The grief hath left thee, and hath been replaced with thy deep and abiding love. I wit that he touched thee, that he changed thee. Would that I had but known him.

(She touches his cheek tenderly with her hand, a soft smile upon her lips.)

MARY MAGDALENE: Dost thou truly wish that?

JONATHAN: Yea, but of course! I would give all I own of this earth to have the love which thou dost possess within.

MARY MAGDALENE: 'Tis far more than love, my son. 'Tis also joy, and understanding, but above all 'tis the peace of knowing that thou art one with Jesus and his Father. Is 't which thou dost desire?

JONATHAN: More than all else on this earth, do I desire that love and that peace. Tell me how I may find it.

MARY MAGDALENE: Thou dost truly want to possess it, and to know Jesus? For if thou dost truly desire to know him, thou can.

JONATHAN: But how can that be possible?; for thou hast said that Jesus is dead. One cannot know a dead man.

MARY MAGDALENE: Everyone can know Jesus if they do but one simple thing.

JONATHAN: What be that?

MARY MAGDALENE: Thou must believe that he is his Father's Son. For it is through the Father that one may come to know the Son.

JONATHAN: And who be his father?

MARY MAGDALENE: God.

JONATHAN: Then . . . then Jesus was the Messiah, the promised one of God?

MARY MAGDALENE: Yes.

JONATHAN: And he is dead? But how?

MARY MAGDALENE: He was murdered, crucified upon the cross.

JONATHAN: But why? Why would they murder the Messiah?

MARY MAGDALENE: (A tear slowly trickles down her cheek.) They did not believe that Jesus was the Messiah. They did not believe that he was the Son of God, that he was the one promised in the words of the prophets of old. They feared him. They feared his power over the people of the nations. They did not dare face the risk that any one man from Galilee should usurp the power and the authority of the great Caesar. So they murdered him. 'Twas the only way they knew to protect their own vain interests.

JONATHAN: I believe. I truly believe that Jesus was the Messiah. By no other means couldst thou have come to possess such faith and such love. Only through the Messiah could one come by that faith and that love, for the prophets did write that he would come to love and to save the people.

MARY MAGDALENE: And so he did. With all of his being did he love all of us. The sadness is that not all of us accepted that love. Those who refused to accept it are the ones who murdered him. You and I, we can accept his love, and we can love him, if we but open our hearts and our souls to him. Ask for his love, and he shall surely give it thee. Then, and only then, wilt thou come to know the selfsame love, and freedom, and peace which I now know. Wilt thou do this thing?

JONATHAN: Yes. Yes, I shall gladly do it. I shall go now and ask him to share with me his wondrous love. How can one such as I ever hope to repay thee for this kindness you have given me?

MARY MAGDALENE: There is no need for repayment. All I ask of thee, is that thee keep this love within thine heart alway, and that thee tell willingly to any who ask of thee from whence it comes, that Jesus is the answer. Wilt thou promise me that?

JONATHAN: Oh, yes; yes, I promise thee. I shall do for others what thou hast done for me.

MARY MAGDALENE: Then go, my son, go and pray. Go and ask God the Father to give thee the love of his Son, Jesus.

JONATHAN: I will. I thank thee. And I shall pray that God shall alway bless thee.

MARY MAGDALENE: And I too shall pray that God will alway watch over thee.

(She watches as he disappears from sight, then kneels to pray in the lengthening shadows.)

SCENE II

IN THE GARDEN, NEAR THE SEPULCHRE. MARY MAGDALENE AWAKENS TO BRIGHT AND GLORIOUS SUNLIGHT BEAMING DOWN ON HER. 'TIS NOW MORNING; DRAINED AND EXHAUSTED PHYSICALLY AND MENTALLY, SHE HAD FALLEN ASLEEP SOMETIME DURING THE NIGHT. LOOKING OVER HER SHOULDER AT THE SEPULCHRE, SHE SUDDENLY SEES THAT THE STONE HAS BEEN ROLLED AWAY FROM THE ENTRANCE, AND SHE RUSHES TO THE TOMB. LOOKING IN, SHE FINDS THAT IT IS EMPTY, SAVE FOR THE BRIGHT LIGHT SHINING FORTH FROM WITHIN.

MARY MAGDALENE: My Lord, what have they done with thee?

ANGELS: Woman, why weepest thou so?

MARY MAGDALENE: Because they have taken away the body of my Lord, and to where I know not. Is 't not enough grief I suffered when he was murdered and taken from me thusly?; but to have his body, his earthly remains, so cruelly stolen from the sepulcher where he rested in death, that is more pain than I can yet bear.

(She turns from the tomb, to see a man standing near to where she had kept her sad vigil. She recognizes this man not, for he is covered, his cloke hiding his face in shadows.)

JESUS: Woman, why weepest thou? Whom seekest thou?

MARY MAGDALENE: Sir, pray tell me what thou hast done with him, whereto thou hast taken him. Tell me, and I will but take him from thence and return him to the sepulcher.

JESUS: Mary.

MARY MAGDALENE: Master! (She rushes to him, kneeling at his feet and reaching for him.)

JESUS: Touch me not; for I am not yet ascended to my Father. But go to my brethren, and say unto them, I ascend unto my Father, and your Father; and to my God, and your God.

MARY MAGDALENE: As you desire, Master, so shall I do.

SCENE III

THE HOUSE WHEREIN ARE GATHERED ELEVEN OF THE TWELVE, THOMAS BEING ABSENT.

MARY MAGDALENE: Mourn ye not, for the Lord hath risen from the sepulcher. He is yet alive!

PETER: Woman, what sayest thou? How can Jesus be alive, risen from the tomb, when we, all of us, saw him hanged from the cross and dead? Didst thou not witness his death same as we?

MARY MAGDALENE: Thou knowest that I did. But only just now I saw our Lord, alive and risen from the grave. He did bid me come to thee.

PETER: Now thou sayest that he did speak to thee? What is 't that this vision of yours did say to thee?

MARY MAGDALENE: He did say that I should tell thee that he was to ascend unto his Father, our Father.

PETER: What foolishness! Get thee from before me, woman.

LEVI: Hold thy temper, Peter. Thou knowest that Jesus did love Mary especially. 'Twould not be so strange should he appear to her before he should appear unto us. Do not be so harsh toward her. She would have no cause to lie to us about our Lord, would she? Do not be so ready to doubt her, Peter.

PETER: Thou must admit that her words do sound as if 'twere but an idle tale. 'Tis hard for one to believe such a tale.

MARY MAGDALENE: I blame thee not, Peter, for the doubt thou dost feel. But it should be for those of us who know the Lord to keep his teachings and his commandments closest to our hearts, and to practice them in our daily lives. We should all be as much like the Lord as is possible for us creatures to be.

SCENE IV

THE EVENING OF THE SAME DAY, IN THE HOUSE OF THE DISCIPLES.

JESUS: Peace be unto you.

(He reveals the wounds in his hands and his side to them.)

PETER: Lord! 'Tis true! Thou art indeed risen from the tomb!

JESUS: Peace be unto you: as my Father hath sent me, even so send I you. Go ye unto all the world, and preach the gospel to every creature.*

THE END

*The words of Jesus are quoted directly from the King James Bible.

WORKS CONSULTED

Benoit, Pierre. <u>The Passion and Resurrection of Jesus Christ</u>. New York: Herder and Herder, 1970.

<u>The Bible</u>. King James Version.

Deen, Edith. <u>The Bible's Legacy for Womanhood</u>. Garden City, NY: Doubleday and Company, 1969.

Gibran, Kahlil. <u>Jesus: The Son of Man: His Words and His Deeds As Told and Recorded By Those Who Knew Him</u>. New York: Alfred A. Knopf, 1928.

Hastings, James, ed. <u>A Dictionary of Christ and the Gospels, Vol. II</u>. New York: Charles Scribner's Sons, 1908.

Kellner, Esther. <u>Mary of Nazareth</u>. New York: Appleton-Century-Crofts, Inc., 1958.

Maus, Cythnia Pearl. <u>Christ and the Fine Arts: An Anthology of Pictures, Poetry, Music, and Stories Centering on the Life of Christ</u>. New York: Harper and Bros. Pub., 1938.

Pagels, Elaine. <u>The Gnostic Gospels</u>. New York: Random House, 1979.

Pollock, John. <u>The Master: A Life of Jesus</u>. Wheaton, IL: Victor Books, 1984.

Robinson, James M., ed. The Nag Hammadi Library in English. San Francisco: Harper and Row Publishers, 1988.

Selvidge, Martha J. Daughters of Jerusalem. Scottdale, PA: Herald Press, 1987.

Swidler, Leonard. Biblical Afflictions of Women. Philadelphia: Westminster Press, 1979.

Templeton, Charles B. Jesus: The Four Gospels, Matthew, Mark, Luke, and John, Combined in One Narrative and Rendered in Modern English. New York: Simon and Schuster, 1973.

Tyson, Joseph B. The New Testament and Early Christianity. New York: Macmillan Publishing Co., 1984.

Webber, F.R. Church Symbolism. Cleveland: J.H. Jansen, 1938.

Sheilah R. Craft is an English professor, writer, blogger, poet, artist, ardent genealogist, and book lover. Born in raised in the Midwestern United States, Sheilah was born surrounded by a close family, including several educators, books, and animals. She began reading and writing very early, and has published short stories, articles, and poems. She is the author of the Christian novel Heart-Glow.

www.ingramcontent.com/pod-product-compliance
Lightning Source LLC
Chambersburg PA
CBHW020302010526
44108CB00037B/519